50 WAYS TO SAVE THE EARTH

Text by **Anne Jankéliowitch**
Photographs by **Philippe Bourseiller**

Abrams Books for Young Readers
New York

50 Ways to Save the Earth

I was twelve when our river was taken from us. I remember it as an act of unimaginable violence. The factories upstream of the village took it upon themselves to empty their chemicals into the water. It was horrible. The river stank. In summer the fish rotted by the ton. It was the end of all our fishing, bathing, boating, and games by the waterside. Everyone suffered. But I don't remember anyone demonstrating or protesting. That was fifty years ago, in a village in southwestern France. We silently submitted to what we thought was the unstoppable march of progress. We didn't worry about nature or people's lives.

In those days there were 2.55 billion inhabitants on the planet, which we thought wasn't affected by the demands we made on it. In just half a century, the world's population has almost tripled. The demand for energy, raw materials (which we also call primary commodities), transport, water, and food has increased tenfold. Today we are reaching the limits of a world we once reckoned inexhaustible. Fifty years is but a moment in the history of humankind. But the speed and scale of our impact are now outstripping the earth's capacity to recover a healthy balance. The threats are everywhere.

Nature is the world's greatest cooperative: All its species—animal and plant, macro- and microscopic—lead interdependent lives. They all contribute to the stability of the world's ecosystems, the biosphere, the oceans, the atmosphere, the climate. It has taken them millions of years to create suitable conditions for mankind to emerge. But it has taken mankind just one short century to not only dominate the earth's surface and species, but endanger its ecological harmony as well.

If we follow the suggestions in this book and carry out the everyday actions outlined here, we will each be able to make a significant difference and impact our planet's future. Let's act now—before the earth takes revenge on us for our disrespect.

Jean-Louis Étienne, Polar Explorer, June 6, 2007

Chapter 1
Putting the Trashcan on a Diet

Buy Reusable

Instead of buying a throwaway product, why not choose to buy the same thing but in reusable form? A washable handkerchief instead of tissues, normal dishware instead of plastic plates and cups, a washcloth instead of wipes (which take a long time to decompose), dish towels instead of paper towels. They create much less waste and harm the planet less.

WHY SO MANY THROWAWAY ITEMS?

Pens, tissues, wipes, cups, paper towels, razors—we use them once, and then off they go! Into the trash! How convenient! But what would the planet say if we asked for its opinion?

The manufacture of all these products uses a lot of natural resources. Just one example: The manufacture of disposable plates uses trees (for cardboard plates) or petroleum (for plastic plates), plus water and the energy needed to drive the machines—not to mention the energy to transport the products to the factory. Every stage contributes to deforestation (lots of trees are felled), to pollution of the water and air (factory discharges contain harmful substances), and to global warming (the energy used emits greenhouse gases). That's a lot of damage and pollution for just a plate, wouldn't you say?

AND THEN WHAT HAPPENS?

Few throwaway objects are recyclable. Once they are in the trashcan, they contribute largely to the quantity of waste that has to be dealt with and hidden away. Our planet is not like a plastic plate or a paper napkin. It's not disposable. There isn't another one for us to use when we've ruined this one!

Idea: Skip the disposable! Buy reusable!

Sort Your Trash

Do you know that when you recycle your aluminum cans, you are helping to conserve nature and natural resources? The same goes for your plastic bottles (less petroleum used), your paper (fewer trees cut down), or steel cans (less iron ore dug out of the ground). Recycling uses less energy than manufacturing from scratch.

HOW DO YOU TURN A HEAP OF PLASTIC BOTTLES INTO A FLEECE JACKET?

And how do you turn shampoo bottles into telephone cards? A wine bottle into a jam jar? Soda cans into a bicycle? Not by magic. But through recycling.

To recycle we first need to sort through what we throw away. Plastic, glass, aluminum, steel, cardboard—they each have their own road to follow! Sorting them is far better than throwing them away. It is a vital stage in the life of a material that will soon serve another use rather than be squandered.

Here's an example. When aluminum cans are recycled, it becomes possible to manufacture aluminum without mining it. Are you aware that to extract bauxite (the mineral that aluminum comes from), enormous open-pit mines are needed that destroy the woodland and animals that live there? So instead of throwing these cans away, always recycle when you can!

In the end, lots of things can be recycled, and if we pay a little attention, we will quickly see that recycling our trash is very useful.

Idea: Sort what you throw away and RECYCLE, RECYCLE, RECYCLE! Another life (or many) awaits your recyclables, thanks to you!

Let's Cut the Packaging

Take a good look at the packaging on the products you buy. Note if the packaging serves no purpose, and if so, leave it on the shelf. If equivalent products exist with less packaging, buy those instead. In the case of shampoos and shower gels, it is better to buy one large bottle than several small ones.

WHY ALL THIS PACKAGING?

Take for example a small square of chocolate. It is not unusual for squares of chocolate to be wrapped in gold or silver paper either individually or in threes, wrapped with others into slabs, and then sealed in a rigid plastic box. The extra layers of packaging do nothing for the taste, but by adding extra packaging the company can charge more for it. All it does is take up room in the trashcan.

Plastic packaging is not just about the waste it makes; producing it has a huge impact on the environment. The manufacture of plastic needs a primary commodity, petroleum, and 1,650 pounds of petroleum have to be pumped out of the ground to make one metric ton of plastic! Before it can become plastic sheeting, that petroleum has to be transported to refineries and on to factories in what can amount to a journey around the world! All those miles contribute to global warming.

It's the same story with the box containing your tube of toothpaste. That too uses natural resources and energy. It too pollutes the air and water. Yet as soon as it comes home from the supermarket, you throw it in the wastebasket. What is the point? It is simply inconvenient trash, often polluting, and rarely recyclable.

Reducing packaging would mean limiting pollution and the waste of resources it causes. It's a good way of taking care of our planet and thinking about those who will live on it after us.

Idea: Choose something with less packaging whenever you can!

The planet's forests are disappearing faster than they can regrow. A piece of woodland as big as a soccer field disappears on average every three seconds. A surface area the size of Greece is lost every year. (source: FAO)

Saving Paper

In order to conserve the planet's natural resources, sort and recycle your paper and cardboard. In your school you could encourage the collection of used paper for recycling. At the start of the new school year, begin by using last year's supplies, like notebooks that are half full, to avoid unnecessary purchases. Opt for paper and folders made out of recycled paper and cardboard.

HOW THE WORLD'S WOODLANDS DISAPPEAR

When you've finished with a newspaper, it's possible you just throw it in the trash. When you go through your magazines and other paper, you probably do the same. But you're making a mistake. These paper products aren't waste. They are a primary commodity!

When you deposit newspapers, magazines, and office paper for recycling, they are shredded, pulped, and turned into recycled paper and cardboard. Every metric ton of recycled paper saves seventeen trees, 5,800 gallons of water, and the equivalent in energy of the 260 gallons of petroleum needed to manufacture new paper.

Recycling old paper is a good thing. But for the recycling chain to work, it needs buyers of recycled paper products at the other end.

Idea: Make an effort to buy recycled products!

Let's Recycle

More than 80 percent of our garbage is incinerated or buried. But that is not an ideal solution. We need to reduce this amount by recycling everything that can be recycled and by using recycling centers to the maximum.

WHY NOT CONVERT GARBAGE INTO ENERGY OR HEATING?

This already happens in incineration plants, where the trash collected by garbage trucks is burned and then the heat produced is used to create energy. Burned garbage takes up much less space, so it might seem an ideal solution. But it isn't. The burning gives off toxic smoke, including dioxins (which cause cancer) and acid gas (which damages woodland). Filters are therefore put in the furnace flues to reduce air pollution, but these, too, become highly contaminated and need to be disposed of.

IF WE CAN'T BURN GARBAGE, WHAT DO WE DO WITH IT?

One solution is to use landfills instead: We bury the waste away from human eyes and noses and leave it to quietly rot. But in Europe alone, there are already more than a billion metric tons of garbage in landfill sites, and these sites are getting filled up. In any case, they pollute the groundwater, as they don't all have modern linings around them to stop poisonous substances from seeping out. And they contribute to global warming because they give off methane, a greenhouse gas that is produced by decomposition. So the real solution is to recover the garbage and treat it according to the materials it contains. Old refrigerators are a good example. They contain refrigerant gases like Freon, which contribute to global warming if they are allowed to escape into the atmosphere.

Idea: Recycle anything and everything that you can. Recycling is not just about paper and plastic anymore; it's about finding a way to give new life to nearly everything you use.

If the rate of world economic growth does not slow down, energy consumption in 2030 will increase by half its current level. What's really troubling about this is that 87 percent of the energy we use now throughout the world comes from nonrenewable sources, meaning that once we've used it, it's gone forever. (source: International Energy Agency)

Collect Old Batteries

Old batteries are extremely toxic and should never be thrown into the trashcan with other household garbage. Make sure you put them in the special bins provided in supermarkets and other public places. Or better yet, use rechargeable batteries! There will be fewer to throw away and it's cheaper!

WHAT'S THE FUTURE FOR BATTERIES?

Batteries power watches, toys, flashlights, iPods, and a lot more, as if by magic! But inside a battery there's a lot going on—a chemical reaction that releases energy in the form of electricity. It uses metals like cadmium, mercury, lead, nickel, zinc, or manganese. The trouble is that all these things are toxic and dangerous to the environment. Just one round mercury battery no bigger than a button will, if dumped in the natural environment, pollute more than one hundred gallons of water and a cubic meter of ground for fifty years.

Luckily, we know how to treat the harmful products of used batteries and can recycle them in specialized factories. Furnaces are heated to 2,192 degrees Fahrenheit to melt the batteries and recover their heavy metals, so that the metals can be used again. Ferromanganese, for example, can be reused in the making of faucets or taps as well as railroad rails. Zinc is reused in the making of guttering and antirust paints. When you recycle a battery, you aren't just avoiding pollution of the environment; you're also preventing the squandering of expensive, nonrenewable primary commodities.

Idea: Always recycle your batteries!

Avoid Plastic Bags

When you go shopping, don't forget to take reusable bags with you. They're bigger, tougher, and can be used dozens of times, which saves hundreds of throwaway plastic bags from our trashcans and from the environment. Whenever a store clerk puts something in a plastic bag, think about it for a second: Do you really need a bag for that pack of gum that could go in your pocket?

WHAT'S THE IMPACT OF A PLASTIC BAG?

Where'd that plastic bag come from? The wind took it. Maybe a day ago it was in your hand. Too many stores hand out plastic bags. Every year in the United States, 380 billion plastic bags end up in the trash. That's ridiculous! And that is why some supermarkets have decided to replace them with reusable bags.

SO WHY ARE THEY STILL MAKING SO MANY BAGS?

The average American uses three hundred to seven hundred plastic bags per year, most of which end up in landfills, and on top of it all, it takes an estimated 12 million barrels of oil to make those bags! And the plastic degrades very slowly: A single-use plastic bag made out of polyethylene takes approximately one thousand years to degrade.

Idea: Do your part and use a canvas bag, or reuse the plastic bags you've already taken.

This is the story of a sea turtle swimming peacefully in the ocean. It thinks that what it sees before it is a translucent jellyfish—a tasty meal. But what it swallows doesn't really feel like a jellyfish . . . No, it's a plastic bag that was simply floating there. The turtle was mistaken. It will die, suffocated. Its fate is not uncommon; many thousands of whales, turtles, birds, and other wildlife die because of plastic bags.

Operation Recovery!

Encourage everyone in your family to put their discarded cell phones in the facilities designed for safely disposing of them. Some of your old cell phones can be repaired, reconditioned, and resold, while others can be recycled so that their toxic materials are recovered and reused.

WHAT'S IN A CELL PHONE?

Lead, cadmium, mercury, chromium, bromide, arsenic, and unrecyclable plastic. In other words, heavy metals and chemicals that may contaminate soil and water. The millions of cell phones cluttering up drawers or thrown into trashcans are a waste of materials and a pollution threat to the environment. And when you think that more than 140 million Americans have cell phones and that most replace their phones every two years, you understand what a great problem this is. It's actually very easy to recycle cell phones; most of the time you can take your cell phone back to the place you bought it and the store will recycle it for you.

It's the same problem with empty printer cartridges. These too endanger the environment if they are not recovered, as the ink residues contain chemical pigments with a cyanide base.

WHO RECYCLES INK CARTRIDGES?

Most ink cartridge manufacturers accept empty cartridges whenever new ones are purchased. A number of charities also collect them to raise money for their work. So make sure all empty cartridges are recycled, both at home and in school. And don't forget that you can use less of them. Some printers have "eco" settings, and if you use the "eco" button, you'll use less ink and produce fewer empty cartridges.

Idea: Get more mileage from your ink cartridge and your cell phone—reuse and then recycle them!

Since 1950, fishing has increased fivefold. Every year, seven million metric tons of fish, turtles, birds, and marine mammals die from being trapped in fishing nets. (source: WWF)

△ One-fifth of the world's coral reefs have been destroyed in less than one hundred years, and half the remaining reefs are threatened by global warming. (source: United Nations Environment Program)

▷ By composting, we could significantly reduce the amount of kitchen waste needing treatment by local authorities. If we add food waste to everything else that is recyclable, then half the contents of our garbage cans would become useful and have a second life. (source: ADEME—French Agency for Environment and Energy Management)

Let's Compost Vegetable Waste

Do you want to do some recycling of your own? Just put some vegetable waste in a covered heap in your garden and let the worms and microorganisms do the rest! In several weeks you'll have some natural fertilizer—compost— which is great for the soil and for plants.

HOW DOES NATURE RECYCLE HER OWN GARBAGE?

Have you noticed that dead leaves and twigs fall on the ground and then quietly rot away until they almost disappear? How do they do this? They are attacked by organisms that live in the soil, like fungi, insects, worms, and bacteria. Just one tablespoon of woodland soil contains more than fifty billion of these organisms! They all work to process plant detritus into humus, natural compost that enriches the soil. That's what composting is all about.

Large factories that make compost from vegetable matter are only reproducing Nature's invention on an industrial scale. But you can also produce compost at home by using the biodegradable waste that makes up a quarter of domestic garbage: garden leaves, mowed grass, vegetable peelings, coffee grounds, tea bags, eggshells, stale bread, and the like.

All that composting clears more room in our trashcans—and it gives us something useful too: an excellent fertilizer! Compost has another advantage: It doesn't pollute, unlike chemical fertilizers, which seep into the water supply. If you don't have enough room at home to make compost, maybe you could ask what they do at school. Do they compost the school's kitchen waste, for example? If not, work with your principal or teacher to get a composting program started.

Idea: Start to compost, either at home or at school!

Take Back Unused Medicines

Don't leave your unused medicine in the medicine chest once you're better. Take it back to the pharmacist. The leftover medicine could be used to treat other sick people.

HOW ARE MEDICINES PRODUCED?

The production of all medicines uses up natural resources. Making 2 1/4 pounds of streptomycin, for example, uses about a thousand gallons of water. Think of the planet—and also of the thirty thousand people who die every year because they lack proper medicines.

WHAT CAN WE DO?

In certain states laws have been passed to allow the recycling of medications. At the time this book went to press Oklahoma, North Carolina, Louisiana, Ohio, Missouri, California, Texas, and Nebraska all had medicine recycling programs in place, while twenty-six other states were awaiting legislation to legalize similar programs. Humanitarian organizations in these states collect unused medication and redistribute it to the most needy here and abroad. These programs have proven to be very effective; in France, for example, twenty million boxes of medication were redistributed in 2003 alone. The impact is huge, because not only are you saving the natural resources it took to produce the medications in the first place, you're also helping those who don't have medicine readily available to them.

Even out-of-date medicines, which cannot be redistributed, should be taken back to the pharmacist, so that they can be destroyed under the best conditions. Accompanying leaflets, cardboard boxes, glass bottles, plastic and aluminum tubes, and aerosols are all recoverable, and can be either recycled or incinerated to produce heating and lighting.

Idea: Recycle your unused medicines or petition your local government to get a program going in your state.

Buy Purpose-Grown Christmas Trees

If you celebrate Christmas, don't hesitate to buy a natural fir or spruce tree: They are grown especially for the occasion and don't contribute to deforestation. Or buy a plastic tree that you can reuse every year.

O CHRISTMAS TREE, O CHRISTMAS TREE . . .

Natural firs and spruces, like all green growing things, absorb carbon dioxide and give out oxygen during their lifetime, which helps in the fight against global warming. So look after them! First of all, before you buy a Christmas tree, see where it comes from. Try to choose one grown locally—these trees travel fewer miles in artificially cooled containers and are better adapted to your region. And opt for one grown without chemical fertilizers and pesticides.

AND AFTER CHRISTMAS?

In some places, if you put your tree out with the garbage cans, it will be taken away and burned with other garbage in an incineration plant. What a waste, when you think about how many other households have also had a tree!

But you could give your tree a second lease on life. You could put it with other green waste where it, too, can be shredded and turned into compost to feed the soil. But it would be better if you could buy a live tree. After New Year, you could plant it in your garden, or that of your grandparents, or alternatively in the countryside where you go for walks. That way you can watch it grow every year!

Idea: Buy locally and purposefully grown Christmas trees.

Let's "Eco-Wrap" During the Holidays!

When the time comes to wrap your presents, think about using recycled paper. Very attractive wrapping can be made from old packaging, such as Tetra Paks (containers for milk, fruit juice, soup, and so on) or from old paper. Honest! Then, instead of throwing everything away, you can sort through it and squirrel away whatever can be used again. It will make your gifts much more interesting!

WHAT ABOUT SOME CLEVER DIY?

The earth doesn't need a big present from you to make it happy during the holiday season. Just do a few things to show you care, and you'll make it the happiest of planets! After the holidays, our trashcans overflow with food packaging, cardboard, and the polystyrene used to protect toys. In just several hours we manage a year's worth of squandering and garbage production! So let's not add—on top of it all—acres of pretty paper ripped to pieces and yards of colored ribbons.

HOW CAN WE LIMIT THE DESTRUCTION?

Quite simply by opening our presents carefully. You could even hold a competition to see who can ruin the least amount of gift wrapping. The pleasure of discovering what's inside the package won't be any less, and you'll be saving the planet's resources as well as your own money. You could make your own decorations for the tree and the house instead of buying new ones every year. But one thing's for sure: You and your family will be surprised at what a noticeable difference a bit of "eco-wrapping" makes!

Idea: Reuse your ribbons and wrapping paper!

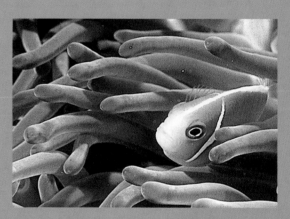

Chapter 2
Saving Endangered Species

Let's Save the Tropical Forests

Buy furniture labeled "FSC" (Forest Stewardship Council), your proof that the wood has come from sustainably managed forests. In those forests only some trees are cut down, and only when they get to the right size. So the lives of the people and animals that live in the forest are respected.

WHAT SPECIES ARE THREATENED BY DEFORESTATION?

Most of the planet's primates—apes, monkeys, and lemurs—live in the tropical forests of Brazil, the Congo, Indonesia, or Madagascar. But in those regions, humans are cutting down trees much faster than new ones can grow. Half of the land has been turned into agricultural plantations or mining sites. So the primates have gone—they have nowhere else to live! Gradually, certain species are disappearing altogether, and a third are in immediate danger of extinction. In less than a hundred years the orangutan will exist only in books.

WHAT ARE WE WAITING FOR?

Everyone agrees. We must stop cutting down tropical forests. We must save the primates. But nobody thinks about that when they buy beautiful teak garden furniture that looks fabulous on the patio, or a mahogany chest of drawers for the living room! It's all made out of tropical hardwood. Maybe it came from trees cut down in Indonesia or Africa, the very trees that, before they were cut down, were home to apes, monkeys, or lemurs.

THERE ARE SOLUTIONS!

Why destroy forests in tropical countries, when it is possible to buy wood from trees growing in our own temperate zones, in sustainably managed forests? If we use the chestnuts, oaks, larches, pines, spruces, beeches, and other plantation trees that grow nearer to home, we won't just be helping to save the tropical forests. We'll also cut out miles and miles of unnecessary and polluting transportation.

Idea: Buy wood and furniture that come from sustainably managed forests.

Print on Both Sides
of the Paper

To economize on paper, use both sides of your white paper, and collect any nonconfidential used paper that your parents bring home from work for scrap paper, shopping lists, and the like. Don't print out your e-mails unless you have to, and add this advice to the foot of your e-mails to encourage your addressees to do the same. One of the advantages of computers is that we don't need to use so much paper!

DO WE REALLY NEED ALL THOSE PLANT SPECIES?

Some species are disappearing. Until now that doesn't seem to have affected our existence much. So what are we worried about? Are they that useful? Well, yes. Particularly where medical science is concerned. Most humans on the planet don't have access to factory-made medicines. They still use plant medicines. Even a quarter of the drugs prescribed by doctors in industrialized countries contain ingredients discovered in plants. Without plants, those treatments would not exist. Ninety percent of the world's plant kingdom remains unexplored, mostly in the tropical rain forests. As we cut down the forests, we may be losing cures for major diseases before we can even discover them. In the forests of Borneo, researchers have identified a potential cure for AIDS in the latex of one tree, while in the bark of another a chemical compound has been discovered that combats malaria.

SO LET'S TAKE ACTION!

In wealthy countries—such as the United States, Japan, and the European countries—huge amounts of paper and cardboard are used. The population is increasing, and consumption is rising along with it. We waste a tremendous amount of cardboard packaging and use three times as much paper as forty years ago. And the amounts keep on rising!

Idea: Fight deforestation by using less paper. Turn used paper into scrap paper for grocery lists and notes!

Take the Strain off the Mailbox

**Is your mailbox overflowing with advertising circulars and newspapers?
That's a gigantic and unnecessary waste of paper!**

HOW MANY SPECIES ARE THERE IN THE PLANET'S FORESTS?

To date we know 1.5 million animal and plant species—out of an estimated total of 15 million. Some of the places they live are being destroyed by human beings, built over, or polluted. For instance, in China, forest clearance has driven the giant panda to the brink of extinction.

HOW SERIOUSLY IS THIS DIVERSITY THREATENED?

If we carry on this way, by 2100 we will have destroyed or polluted so much of the world's natural environments that half of all living species will have disappeared forever. But it's worse than that. No species, even the smallest insect, is here by chance. Every species plays a part in the overall balance of the planet. Bees, for instance, are necessary to our existence. It's not just the honey they make. If they weren't here to pollinate flowers, many plants would be unable to reproduce and would die out. So would some of the animals that eat them. And human beings eat these plants and animals too.

The tropical forests are the richest regions on the planet for the number and diversity of living species. Yet these forests are disappearing before our very eyes. Some of the wood is simply pulped for paper, to produce advertising papers whose life lasts only a few minutes. Ten million trees go directly into the trashcan every year. We need to say "Stop!"—right away.

Idea: If you don't want to share in all the waste, put a sticker on your box saying "Please No Advertising Material" or have your parents unsubscribe to junk mailing lists, which means less annoying junk mail and more relief for the environment!

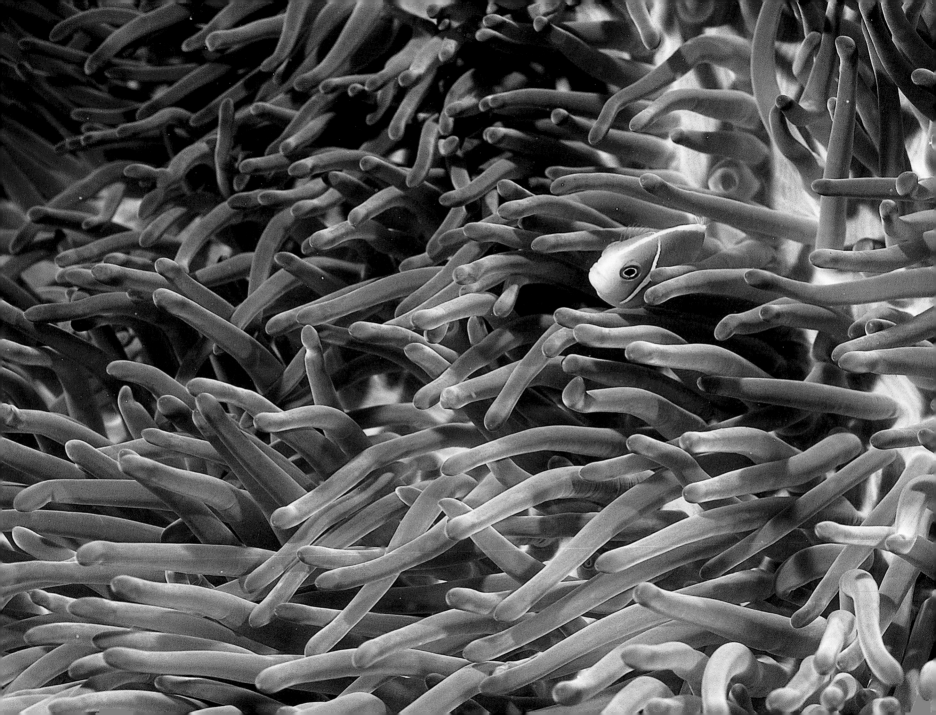

Let's Stop the Traffic in Ivory

When you go on a trip, are you tempted to bring back an animal, a plant, or an object made from an animal as a souvenir? In the future, make sure it's an authorized import. You don't want to help wildlife trafficking without realizing it or contribute to the disappearance of a protected species.

WHY THE CARNAGE?

What have the elephants of Africa done to see their population killed on such a large scale these last few years? Nothing, apart from having tusks on their heads. Between 1975 and 1980, 70,000 elephants were killed every year simply to take their tusks and turn them into ivory jewelry, statuettes, and other ornaments. If the ivory trade hadn't been banned in 1990, all of Africa's elephants would have disappeared forever. There have been similar problems with rhinos (killed for their horns), turtles (their shells are used to make jewelry and spectacles), pythons (their skin is used for handbags, belts, and other accessories), coral (used to decorate aquariums), and many other species whose export is banned.

Under the Convention on International Trade in Endangered Species (CITES), it is illegal to import such objects into the United States or Europe without a license, and this extends to certain plants (orchids, cacti), and living wild animals (parrots, monkeys, snakes). In spite of these measures an illegal trade still goes on. So keep your eyes open!

Idea: Do something locally. Volunteer at a nearby animal shelter!

Currently, worldwide, one in four mammal species are threatened, as are one in eight bird species, one in three fish species, and two in five amphibian species. (source: IUCN—The World Conservation Union)

Travel Ecologically!

When you travel, make sure you obey environmental health regulations. For instance, don't take flowers or foods (such as fruit) to islands. Island environments are more vulnerable to disturbance than mainland ones, and you could unwittingly be the cause of an ecological catastrophe!

HOW CAN ONE PLANT COLONIZE A WHOLE ISLAND?

In 1937 a plant enthusiast brought a small miconia—a beautiful Central American tree with large purple leaves—onto the island of Tahiti to plant in his garden. He didn't realize that he had set off a major ecological disaster. The tree found its adoptive land so congenial that in less than fifty years it spread far and wide, and today covers two-thirds of the island. It drove out the more fragile island species, replacing fruit trees and causing landslides because of its shallow roots—the trees it replaced had deeper roots and held the soil in place better on slopes. The worst of it all is that no one knows how to get rid of it even today.

It's the same story in Africa with the water hyacinth, an aquatic plant that arrived from Brazil a century ago. It has now invaded whole lakes, suffocating the fish that feed the population, hindering navigation, and interfering with the functioning of hydroelectric dams. Cases like this exist all over the world—where foreign, introduced species have completely taken over, eliminating native species and causing big problems for human populations. Invasive species are the second-largest cause of species loss worldwide after habitat destruction due to deforestation.

WHAT PRECAUTIONS CAN WE TAKE TO AVOID SUCH DISASTERS?

Some invasive species are deliberately introduced. But often the invader arrives clandestinely—an insect hidden in fruit, a seed stuck to somebody's shoe, seaweed hooked onto the hull of a merchant ship. That's probably how caulerpa, a tropical seaweed, found its way into the Mediterranean Sea, where it now poses a serious problem: It stunts the growth of other plant species and depletes the animals that use them. Rats probably arrived in New Zealand via the ships that docked there, and they have spread disease across the country and eliminated half the native bird species.

Idea: Don't risk being a walking ecological disaster! Be careful. If, for instance, you're taking your walking shoes abroad with you, clean the soles well before you go!

Counting the Birds

Environmental protection organizations often need ecovolunteers, and there are lots of opportunities to join their projects. Find out about these organizations—they're bound to advertise.

WHY A CENSUS OF BIRDS?

What are they doing, those birdwatchers, as they overlook the lake, hidden away with their binoculars and notebooks, whispering? They're actually on a mission: counting the birds that live there! Every year, large numbers of enthusiasts take part in ornithological census campaigns. These censuses are useful, because they make it possible to estimate the population size and development of particular species—their increase or decrease, state of health, vulnerability—and identify the important environments for their survival. You need data like that if you intend to protect a species.

WHAT CAN ORDINARY PEOPLE DO TO HELP?

Other people take on jobs like cleaning up waterways. Equipped with strong boots and gloves, they clear debris and trim the edges to maintain an open, well-aerated environment where diverse and healthy aquatic life can flourish. Elsewhere, volunteers supervise the beaches where sea turtles lay their eggs and protect them from attacks by dogs. Wherever there is an oil spill, energetic volunteers are suddenly needed to clean the shorelines and try to save affected birds and seals.

You too would be welcome if you wanted to care for the natural environment, clean it up, or monitor it. At the same time you would get to know your natural surroundings better and therefore learn how to better protect it.

Idea: Be an ecovolunteer! Help is always welcome.

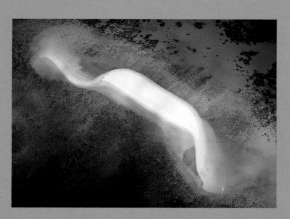

Chapter 3
Showing Respect for Nature

Put Your Litter in the Trashcan

Don't ever discard litter in the natural environment. Keep it with you, in your bag or pocket, until you can find a trashcan. And if there's not one around, keep it until you get home!

WHAT HAPPENS TO OUR LITTER?

When you want to get rid of something—a piece of chewing gum, a tissue, a soda can—and there isn't a trashcan handy, it's tempting to drop it somewhere discreet or throw it out the window. Going, going . . . gone!

Only it hasn't gone anywhere! Dumped in nature, a paper tissue takes three months to degrade, a bus ticket four months, chewing gum five years, an empty soda can ten years, a plastic bottle five hundred years, and a glass bottle much longer than that! You think you've gotten rid of it, but you'll probably rediscover your rubbish next time you pass by the spot. Trash like that doesn't just spoil the look of the natural environment; some of it becomes toxic as it decomposes, polluting the air, the waterways, and the soil. A discarded battery, for instance, leaks acids and heavy metals that poison everything around it.

Other rubbish is dangerous because it can injure—broken glass on a beach, for example—or even kill. Several years ago a whale washed up in Corsica. It had died because of a large plastic tarpaulin that was later found in its stomach. Just remember: Nature isn't a trashcan!

Idea: Hold on to your garbage until you can properly dispose of it.

Leave the Animals in Peace

Always keep your distance from wild animals. Don't stroke them, particularly young ones and chicks. Don't let your odor get onto them. Otherwise, when the parents return, they may not recognize them as their offspring and may reject them.

CAN HUMAN BEINGS AFFECT ANIMAL BEHAVIOR?

In a U.S. national park, the bears gradually got used to having visitors around. They started pilfering food from hikers, becoming more and more daring and eventually aggressive and dangerous. The answer was to allow them to recultivate their natural distrust of humans, to make them keep their natural distance, and to stop hikers from putting food anywhere near them. The rangers used other means to deter the bears from approaching people. They offered them bad-tasting food and scared them whenever they came too close. What a pity it had to come to this!

WHY IS IT SO IMPORTANT NOT TO DISTURB THEM?

When we're in a nature reserve or walking in the countryside, we need to respect wildlife. Don't try to attract animals with food. Our food is not suitable for them. And if they get used to being fed, they may lose the ability to feed themselves and may starve as a result.

Touching wild animals can also endanger their health—and endanger ours—through the transmission of disease. For example, bovine TB (which affects antelopes and deer) can be caught by humans.

Remind yourself: It's when you observe animals from a distance, undetected, that you learn the most about them.

Idea: Leave the animals alone in their natural habitats! Don't feed them or touch them.

Say "No" to Cigarettes

Every year over twelve million acres of forest are used as fuel to dry tobacco. If any of your friends smoke and they aren't bothered about the health risks, just tell them you want a planet that's full of trees!

TOBACCO IS A BIG CONSUMER OF TREES!

Trees, like all plants, help to make the atmosphere breathable, because they absorb carbon dioxide and give out oxygen. That's why they are often nicknamed "the planet's lungs." So cutting down forest to dry tobacco doesn't just damage the lungs of smokers; it affects the earth's own lungs and has consequences for the survival of the human species.

Another thing: The trunks and roots of forest trees hold topsoil in place and help rainwater soak into the earth and replenish the groundwater. Otherwise it rushes over the surface and discharges in abnormally high quantities into the rivers, causing floods. So trees are a first-line flood defense! In Madagascar, so much forest has been cut down that now, every time it rains, the hillsides turn into torrents of mud that slide down into the sea. The villagers are seeing their lands disappear before their very eyes.

FORESTS: THE WORLD'S GREAT STOREHOUSES

Because they contain so many insect, plant, and animal species, the tropical forests are great reserves of biodiversity. Some of these species could help us improve our agriculture (for example, by crossing cultivated species with wild species that have better disease resistance) or help us find new medicines (like a fungus in the Congo that may cure diabetes).

If they are exploited sustainably, the world's forests will also be able to go on supplying wood, which is both an essential building material and a fuel source for a third of the world's population.

Idea: Smoking is bad for your health and the environment. Just say "No" to cigarettes!

Nature reserves and national parks have been established to protect nature and its plants and animals. But they still only account for 9 percent of the earth's surface. And that's not enough. (source: United Nations Environment Programme)

The tropical forests contain half the living species on the planet and supply a major part of the oxygen we breathe. But that isn't going to last: By 2050 half the Amazonian forest will be gone. (source: WWF)

Let's Not Damage the Plants

When you are walking in the wilderness or countryside, keep to the regulated pathways, so as not to damage the plants that are growing all around you. And keep your dog on a leash, so that he doesn't frighten the wildlife.

PLEASE DON'T TOUCH!

Human beings have a strange compulsion to touch the things they look at. That's proved by all those PLEASE DON'T TOUCH signs you see in museums. It's the same in the natural world—the unfortunate ten-dency of people to want to approach wild animals, pick wild-flowers, and move stones or dead wood. Often, what seem like harmless actions do real damage.

For example, if you carve your initials on a tree, you may be pleased to have left your mark. But the tree is alive. Its bark is a bit like our skin: It protects the tree from microbes, fungus infections, and parasites. If you harm its protective layer, you create an open door for diseases that may cause it to drop its leaves and die. Not to mention that those who come after you might not want to look at your initials!

When you pick a wildflower, you disturb the plant's life cycle. You prevent the formation of its seeds, which would have enabled other plants of that species to grow. There are literally hundreds of endangered plant species across North America, and it is strictly forbidden to pick them. The trouble is that not everyone recognizes them. So it's better not to pick any!

Nature isn't a theme park. It's really vulnerable. What it needs is for us to try to experience it without leaving traces of our passage and to respect the rules and guidelines of the sites we visit.

Idea: Respect nature and leave it be.

Gardening Ecologically

It's easy to get a garden in good shape. As much as possible, use natural products, like nettle liquid fertilizer or bordeaux mixture (a natural fungicide). And say "No" to pesticides!

WHY ARE CHEMICAL FERTILIZERS AND HERBICIDES SO HARMFUL?

Farmers are often criticized for polluting rivers with their chemicals. But gardeners are responsible too. A garden is like a field in miniature. There are millions and millions of gardens in the world. To rid their vegetable patches of insects, many gardeners use insecticides. To get rid of the weeds that invade their flowerbeds and restrict plant growth, they use herbicides. These products can be very effective, but they have serious side effects. If overused, they kill the bacteria, fungi, and insects in the soil that break down organic matter (like dead leaves) and release valuable nutrients necessary for plant growth. Insecticides sometimes kill useful insects that eat harmful ones. Both ladybugs and earwigs feed on insects that harm garden plants. If the beneficial insects die, the harmful ones have no natural enemy and can multiply faster, making the problem worse. The gardener may end up adding still more chemicals in an attempt to keep up!

WHERE DO ALL THE CHEMICALS GO?

When it rains, the chemicals wash away into the soil and enter the groundwater. But this is where much of our drinking water comes from. Once these resources are contaminated, they cannot be used—which is a problem, because we need water to live.

One way of breaking out of the vicious cycle is to use biological controls. To get rid of a harmful insect it makes sense to increase the numbers of its natural predator. The ladybugs would love to feast on the aphids destroying your garden's roses! And it's an efficient and natural way for you to deal with them.

Idea: Garden smart; don't use harmful pesticides!

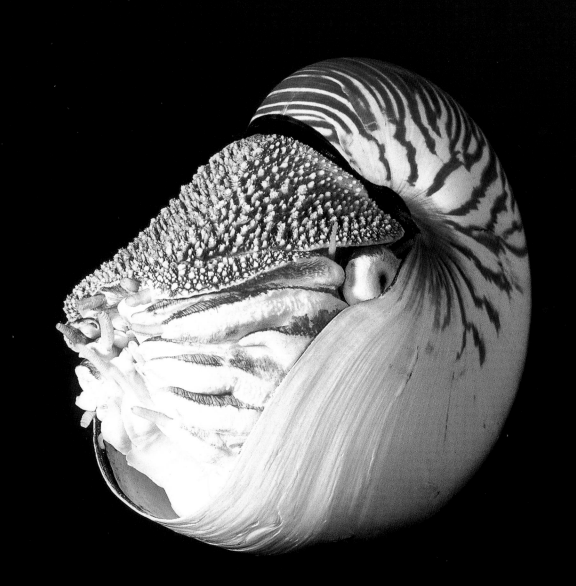

Leave Shore Life Alone

When you're at the beach, fight the urge to collect shellfish, which always end up in the garbage because of their bad smell! And always put back the stones and empty shells in tide pools as you find them—they are probably the home of some timid animal.

DO YOU REALIZE THAT A SEASHELL IS A SORT OF HOUSE? The seashore is fascinating. There's always so much to look at! In the hollow of the rocks, in a puddle, on the sand, under the water—a host of animals live there. But most of those animals are tiny and fragile and don't like to be disturbed. Imagine a giant coming and turning your house upside down to see what's underneath and leaving it like that! You'd have to abandon it, wouldn't you?

In tropical places, there is often coral, which you can see when you swim underwater. You should never break bits off for souvenirs. It may look like rock, but it's really alive and incredibly slow-growing. What can be broken off in a moment or two probably took decades to grow and plays an important part in maintaining the equilibrium of the oceans. It's where many sea creatures live, feed, find shelter to breed and bring up their young, hide from predators, or alternatively lurk for prey. All those shells and the corals that form the reefs, therefore, need to stay in the sea—not least of all because they are home to species of fish and marine creatures that are an important source of food for human beings. That's another good reason for us to leave their living environment intact.

Idea: Leave coral and seashells in place, where nature intended them to be.

Celebrating the Earth!

Why not show appreciation for your planet by joining in the many events that celebrate it—Earth Day, World Environment Day, World Ocean Day, World Carfree Day— or participating in one of the many special rides organized across the globe to promote bike use?

HOW IS LIFE ON EARTH POSSIBLE?

Earth is the only planet that fulfills all the conditions needed for life—or at least it's the only one we know about! One thing that makes the planet Earth livable is that it has water, which all living things need. It also has an atmosphere, which works with the sun to make sure that Earth's temperatures aren't extreme like those of other planets (either burning hot or freezing cold). The atmosphere contains air that is breathed by all living things—plants, animals, and human beings. Another factor is the fertile soils that make agriculture and livestock farming possible—and don't forget the fish in the sea that feed us too. Earth provides mineral wealth, which we transform into materials that house us and allow us to manufacture the things we need. Finally, the planet provides the energy we need to light our homes, power our factories, and move people and things about. These are all services that the natural world provides for nothing. We take the earth so much for granted that we tend to forget that we owe it for *everything* it does to sustain our life.

WHEN CAN WE SAY "THANK YOU"?

All year round. There's nothing stopping you from visiting botanical gardens, environmental centers, aquariums, nature reserves, or national parks, depending on the season. Or you can join associations that organize walks and trips to explore a site or observe animals in the company of people that are enthusiastic about them. There are millions of opportunities and ways to learn about the natural world that sustains us, to become more aware of its importance, and to figure out how to better protect it.

Idea: Get active! Participate in protecting the environment any way you can, even if it's through celebration!

Chapter 4
Economizing Energy

Global warming is increasing the volume of the oceans, melting glaciers, and raising sea levels. There could be a sea level rise of at least four inches (maybe a lot more) before 2100. For Venice, the Netherlands, the low-lying islands in the Pacific, and even the coasts of the United States, this means certain flooding and an inevitable exodus to other countries and cities. (source: United Nations Environment Programme)

Let's Not Waste Energy

Looking for tips on ways to save electricity? Switch off the lights whenever you leave a room, avoid unnecessary lighting, and put your desk under a window to benefit from daylight. Equip the house with low-energy compact fluorescent lightbulbs (CFLs). They use much less electricity and last seven times as long as conventional bulbs.

WHAT IS HAPPENING TO OUR PLANET'S CLIMATE?

It's heating up. And that's causing huge changes on the earth's surface. One of these changes is a rise in sea level, due mainly to thermal expansion of the oceans. Quite simply, as water warms up, it takes up more room. To a lesser extent, sea level rise is also linked to the melting of glaciers at the earth's poles and on mountains. So the oceans could be more than three feet higher a century from now! The wetlands of Louisiana and the Netherlands could disappear. Bangladesh, where millions live, could be swamped, and so could many small islands. That would create a lot of refugees.

BUT WHY IS THE EARTH HEATING UP ABNORMALLY?

The earth is protected by its atmosphere, which contains gases that produce a greenhouse effect: They trap heat close to the earth, just as glass traps heat in a greenhouse. This is a good thing. If those gases weren't there, the temperature on Earth would on average be -64 degrees Fahrenheit! But over the past century, people have used more and more energy for electricity, heating, and transport—energy that comes from petroleum, natural gas, or coal. These energy sources also produce greenhouse gases, so they add to the gases that are *naturally* there in the atmosphere. So the greenhouse effect is intensified, and the climate heats up *unnaturally*.

Idea: Preserve energy any way you can; switch lights off when you leave the room; buy eco-friendly, long-lasting lightbulbs; and unplug all of your electronics when you go on vacation!

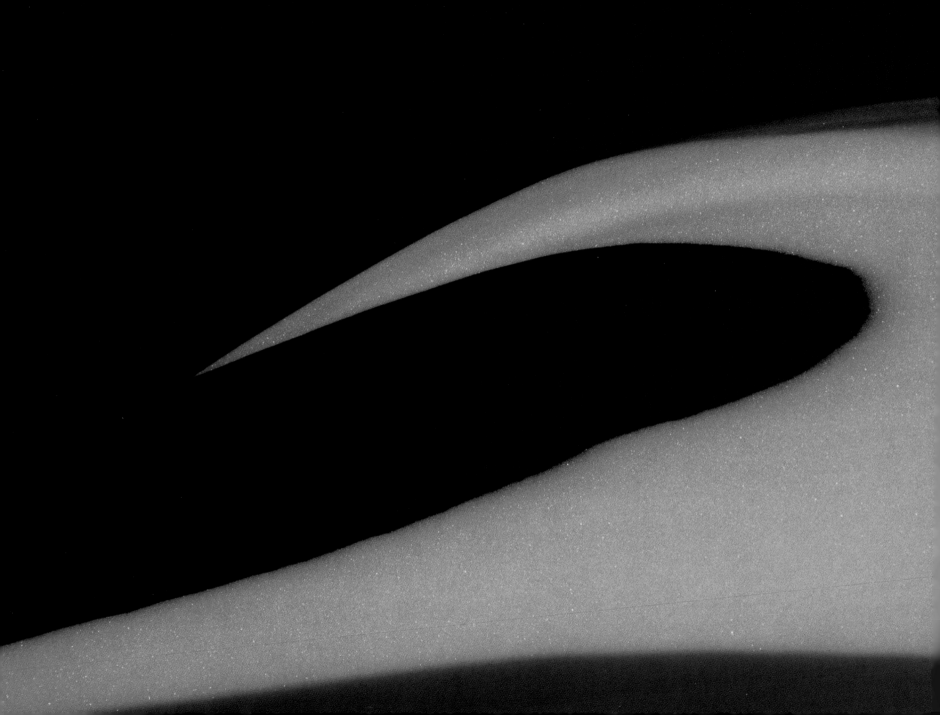

If between now and 2100 the earth's average temperature rises between one and nine degrees Fahrenheit and by thirteen degrees in the polar regions, what will become of the emperor penguins? (source: Intergovernmental Panel on Climate Change)

Avoid Air-Conditioning

When it's hot in summer, plug in your fan: It uses ten times less energy than air-conditioning. Close blinds and shutters—another way to keep out the heat that uses no energy at all.

DO YOU KNOW WHAT DETERMINES GLOBAL GEOGRAPHY . . .

. . . and the extent of the deserts, the distribution of the forests, and the presence of glaciers? It's the world climate! So if the temperatures change at surface level on the earth, all these big regions will change too. Scientists are finding it difficult to estimate what the world will look like in a hundred or two hundred years, because they don't know what the extent of global warming will be. They can only suggest that certain mountain glaciers will disappear, that lots of ski resorts will lose their snow, that dry regions will get even less rainfall, and that malaria outbreaks will increase in southern Europe because the higher temperatures there will favor mosquitoes.

What is certain, though, is that every natural environment contains a certain number of species. If these species are impacted, disappear, or are displaced elsewhere, many of their associated species will not survive: Either they won't be quick enough to follow or adapt, or there will be nowhere to go. What will polar bears do when the ice sheets are too thin to bear their weight? Turn themselves into forest bears over several generations? Impossible. It's much more likely that they'll simply die out. And they won't be alone. Some researchers estimate that by 2050 one-fifth of today's species will have vanished from the earth.

WHO'S RESPONSIBLE FOR THIS MESS?

No doubt about it—it's us. Because it's human activity that produced the extra greenhouse gases that have led to global warming. The increasing tendency to switch on the air conditioner is a good illustration, because air-conditioning is particularly energy-greedy.

Idea: Try to dissuade your parents from installing air-conditioning at home, and keep yourself cool by staying close to the fan!

Try Carpooling

Today, in cities, most automobiles travel with just one person inside. That creates a lot of congestion on the highways and wasted fuel. Carpooling means joining with two or more people who are going to the same place. For example, if you go to school by car, and one of your fellow students lives nearby, why should you use two vehicles every day when you could just take one?

HOW CAN HUMAN BEINGS BE RESPONSIBLE FOR SOME NATURAL DISASTERS?

One of the probable effects of global warming is thought to be that natural disasters will increase in intensity and frequency. And the practical modifications that people have made to their surroundings can make natural events even harder to cope with. For example, the ground absorbs less floodwater when it has been covered with concrete and asphalt or where trees have been removed: When it rains heavily, the water runs immediately into the waterways, causing them to overflow within hours. The results are all the more disastrous because so many homes are built in vulnerable areas close to rivers.

HOW DO THESE CONSEQUENCES AFFECT PEOPLE?

Each time there is a major flood or tornado, thousands of people find themselves homeless. In a matter of hours they may lose everything they have, and may be thankful still to be alive. It's hard to imagine that when you're sitting peacefully and comfortably at home.

No one can do anything about a flood or storm once it's arrived. But we can all stop extreme events from becoming more frequent. We can't bridle the physical forces of nature, but we can all do something to limit climate change—by living differently!

Idea: Carpool, carpool, carpool! Or better yet, take public transportation!

Avoid Using Standby Settings

Here's something simple and easy to remember. Don't leave your computer or printer on standby when they're not in use. And be sure to turn off idle electrical equipment in the living room. The average television set is watched for only four hours a day. Yet if left on standby for the remaining twenty hours, it will use just as much electricity!

HOW MUCH DO YOU KNOW ABOUT "RENEWABLE" ENERGY?

There are many energy sources that, unlike petroleum, produce electricity without warming the climate. Wind energy (using wind turbines), solar energy (using solar panels), hydropower (where water drives turbines in dams or turbines connected to wheels), and geothermal energy (harnessing the natural heat below the ground)—none of these discharge greenhouse gases into the atmosphere and affect the climate.

DO THESE ENERGY SOURCES HAVE OTHER ADVANTAGES?

Yes. They don't pollute the atmosphere like most of today's power stations, do not produce radioactive waste (as nuclear power plants do), and will not run out. Fossil fuels like gas, coal, and petroleum are taken from reserves under the ground. In fifty years' time, petroleum will become scarce, and eventually there won't be any left! At some point we'll be forced to find alternatives. But can the climate wait that long? Unfortunately, at present the world's richest countries continue to buy petroleum—because it is still relatively cheap—rather than make the more expensive investments in research and development that will enable renewable energy to be produced as cheaply as today's fossil fuels.

But while we wait for renewable energy to become readily available, don't forget that the electricity that pollutes the most is the one we currently use!

Idea: Turn your electronics off. ALWAYS!

Turn Down the Heat!

In the winter, try not to heat your house or classroom so much. Instead, put on a sweater or sweatshirt. Turn down or switch off the heating when you open a window or go out of the room. At night, turn the heating down—sixty-four degrees Fahrenheit is quite sufficient—and slide beneath some good covers. It's actually healthier, and you'll sleep better!

WHAT'S SO IMPORTANT ABOUT CORAL REEFS?

The world's coral reefs abound with life. A multitude of sea creatures depend on them for a place to reproduce, protect their offspring, feed, and hide. If the coral dies, all its inhabitants, especially its many fish, decline. Every year, thousands of coral polyps—the little animals, several millimeters long, that build the coral reefs in tropical seas—die as a result of global warming, and no one gives it much thought. That's a pity, because coral plays an important role in maintaining the balance in the oceans.

Coral is very sensitive to changes in the temperature of the water. The climatic changes of the last few years have slightly raised sea temperatures in certain tropical regions. This has been enough to kill a lot of coral. And when coral dies, it takes years for it to replenish.

The coral reefs may seem way beyond our reach, but everything we do here to limit global warming has an impact thousands of miles away, and even impacts the coral. All transport, automobile use especially, affects the climate. Our homes, too, especially how much we heat them. The less heating we use, the less energy is consumed, which, in turn, means fewer greenhouse gases produced and less artificial warming of the climate.

Idea: Lower the thermostat and save the coral!

There's room for all the species that live on the earth—plant, animal, and human. But if all the humans on the planet adopted our Western lifestyle, we'd need two extra planets to satisfy them. (source: WWF)

Try Eating Locally And Seasonally

You can't do better than fruit and vegetables that are grown close to where you live. They will be in better shape, are better for you, and their arrival on your table won't be so troublesome to the planet. So, when you shop, look to find out where the fruit and vegetables you buy have come from.

IN WHAT SEASON DO STRAWBERRIES RIPEN?

And apples? And apricots? Answer: All year round, on supermarket shelves! But that's not Nature's doing. Nature needs a particular season, when the heat and light are right. So how come we find so many fruits and vegetables out of season in our stores?

Some are produced by artificial growing systems, heated greenhouses, for instance, which consume large quantities of water, energy, and raw materials.

Others come from afar, from distant countries where those fruits and vegetables are in season. In European supermarkets you can find green beans from Kenya, carrots from Israel, apples from Australia, and kiwis from New Zealand. Their transport, particularly by air, represents a considerable expenditure of energy, adds to pollution, and contributes to climate change.

Idea: Eating locally grown produce can make a big difference. Buy and eat local foods when you can.

Let's Protect the Atmosphere

Plant a tree whenever you get the chance. That way you will be helping to protect the atmosphere from excessive carbon dioxide and also to counteract deforestation.

WHAT IS RESPONSIBLE FOR GLOBAL WARMING?

The main factor is the emission of excessive amounts of carbon dioxide (CO_2) through various human activities. Every year human beings produce about seven billion metric tons of CO_2, mainly through transportation and industry. But it doesn't all end up in the atmosphere. Only three billion metric tons of it can be detected in the atmosphere. So where are those missing four billion metric tons?

The answer is that they end up in the oceans and trees. The oceans absorb about two billion tons of carbon in the form of gas that dissolves in their waters: This is a wholly natural and normal process. The other two billion tons are absorbed by the planet's plant life, especially the forests. Whereas human beings breathe in oxygen and breathe out carbon dioxide, trees do the opposite: They take in carbon dioxide (not least of all what we breathe out) and exchange it for oxygen. This is part of the process called photosynthesis. The forests are therefore a biological lung that is essential to human beings' survival. Photosynthesis is the air purification system that provides us with the air we breathe! Over time the forests also become huge stockpiles of carbon in the form of wood.

The forests therefore help to limit the greenhouse effect that is causing global warming. For example, roughly two and a half acres of forest absorb the carbon emissions produced by one hundred average-size cars in a year.

Idea: Trap some carbon. Plant some trees.

Chapter 5
Caring for Water

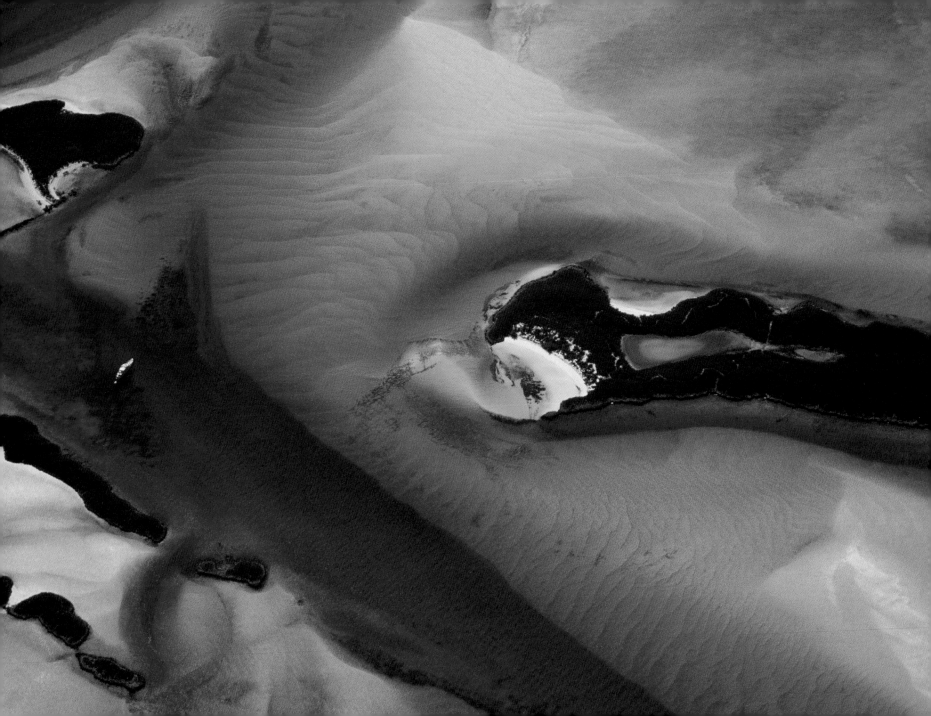

Freshwater is not plentifully available everywhere, and its total quantity worldwide is limited. Since 1950 world consumption of freshwater has risen sixfold, and by 2025 some 2.4 billion people could be without it. (source: C.I.EAU, France)

Let's End River Pollution

Don't throw your litter into gutters or streams. The rain is likely to transport it to the nearest river.

WHAT ARE THE EFFECTS OF CHEMICALS ON RIVERS?

To get their crops to grow faster, farmers often feed their plants with fertilizer containing nitrogen, a nutrient essential to plant growth. But in general they add more than the plants can actually use, and it gets washed away by the rain and ends up in nearby rivers. There the extra nitrogen promotes the growth of other, less benign plants. In particular, well-fed algae start to grow out of control and take up all the oxygen, space, and other nutrients in the river. Gradually the other aquatic species are choked and they disappear. This phenomenon is known as eutrophication, and it can wreak havoc on rivers and lakes.

Sometimes, the places where rivers enter the sea are troubled by this artificial enrichment of the water, and there is a proliferation of seaweed, which then washes up in massive quantities on the shoreline. Here the weed doesn't just create inconvenience because it has to be removed; it also damages the regular marine plants and animals there.

In addition to excessive amounts of fertilizer, rivers are also polluted by chemical waste. A quarter of Western Europe's rivers are so degraded that they are reckoned to be biologically dead: Nothing lives in them.

Idea: When you feel tempted to throw things in the gutter, don't forget that it probably leads straight to the nearest river! Don't litter!

Don't Leave the Water Running!

When you brush your teeth or wash your hands, don't leave the water running. In three minutes, you'll probably have saved four and a half gallons of water—think how many bottles of water that is. And if possible, take a shower (six and a half to twenty-one gallons of water) rather than a bath (fifty-two to sixty-six gallons).

HOW MUCH WATER DO WE HAVE?

When you live on a planet nicknamed "The Blue Planet," you wouldn't expect to fear a shortage of water. But although there is a lot of water on Earth, most of it is salty, and only a tiny proportion is freshwater that human beings can drink. To picture this, imagine that all the water in the sea could fit into a big bucket. By comparison the freshwater frozen in the world's glaciers and mountain snowcaps would fill a coffee cup. But what is actually available to us in lakes, rivers, and groundwater would fill just a teaspoon!

The problem is not just that there are more and more people to share so little water. It's also that the freshwater available is increasingly polluted by agricultural runoff, industry, and cities. One day, perhaps, clean water, so essential for life, will be so scarce that people will fight over it.

Idea: Water is precious. Let's not waste it. Take shorter showers and don't leave the water running while you brush your teeth!

Wait for the Rain

It is better to wait until evening to water the garden. When plants are out of the sun, they lose less water through evaporation, and their needs are reduced by half. Watch the weather forecast: It's a shame to waste sixty gallons of drinking water (a bathful) if it's going to rain the next day. And use a bucket when you wash the car. Hoses waste an enormous amount of water because of their continuous flow.

HOW FAMILIAR ARE YOU WITH THE WATER CYCLE?

Water falls from the sky in the form of rain. Some of it filters into the groundwater; the rest runs into the rivers and eventually into the sea. Some of the seawater evaporates into the air, leaving the salt behind; the water vapor forms clouds that then condense to fall as rain. All the water we use in our homes, factories, and farms comes from groundwater, lakes, and rivers. And when it has been through our houses, factories, and fields, it goes back to the rivers (some at least having been purified in treatment plants), thereby rejoining the water cycle. The total amount of water on our planet, imprisoned in this everlasting circulatory system, never varies. The water you drank today was probably drunk by dinosaurs millions of years ago! There's never any more and never any less of it on Earth! That's why it's so important not to waste it. Especially if it's been treated for drinking quality, as happens in industrialized countries.

Idea: Don't water the lawn unless it's absolutely necessary! Wait for the rain!

Saving and Recycling Water

Ask your parents to fit the toilets in your house with a dual flush, one that will deliver one or two gallons as required. There's no point in using two gallons where one will do. Alternatively, you could put a brick or a bottle filled with sand in the tank: It's a way of reducing the tank's capacity and therefore the amount of water used per flush.

HOW DO WE GET OUR WATER?

In developed countries it's easy to get water to drink: You just turn on a faucet or tap. You might think it's the same for everybody. But it isn't. Every morning on the planet there are millions of people who have to walk miles with a bucket to get five gallons or so of water from the bottom of a well. Sometimes the water isn't really drinkable—it may cause diseases, possibly fatal ones—but it's the only water those people have, and it needs to last all day.

Five gallons isn't much. Three or four flushes in one of our toilets! And the water we use is of drinking quality. Yet we actually drink only 1 percent of the water we use in our homes. A third of it is used to flush the toilet!

For flushing the toilet, wouldn't it be more sensible to recycle rainwater or water that's already been used for other domestic purposes? They already do that in some parts of Japan. We just need to organize it here.

Idea: Encourage your parents to get a dual flush toilet, or better yet, organize your community and petition to use recycled rainwater in your toilets.

Look at this humpback whale. She swam to the warm waters of the tropics to reproduce. She and her offspring will soon go back to the cold waters of the Southern Ocean to play, sing, and feed. But the route is long and dangerous. Did you know that whales are still threatened by the harpoons of whale hunters who want them for whale meat?

Let's Get Moving Against Oil Spills

Travel by bus, train, or subway, and encourage your parents, or the adults who drive you, to make more use of public transport. A full bus means that around thirty cars stay in their garages. It's the equivalent of a drop less of petroleum in the next oil spill—or even a whole oil spill averted if everybody makes the same effort.

WHY DO OIL SPILLS CAUSE SO MUCH DAMAGE?

Oil spills are caused by accidents to oil tankers as they travel over the world's oceans. Every time an accident occurs near land, miles of coastline and hundreds of sea creatures and birds are covered with oily slime.

Everyone agrees: Oil spills are disgusting and terrible for nature. Everyone blames the oil tankers. But people often forget why there are so many tankers on the surface of the oceans. They're there to feed our demand for energy, which we use, without much thought, to light our homes, keep us warm, power industry, and, last but not least, provide fuel for road vehicles. The roads of Europe, for example, are used by three times as many automobiles as thirty years ago, and in the United States the increase is even more drastic! And they don't get used in a rational way. People use cars for journeys that they could just as well make on foot, by bike, by bus, or by train. That's why there are so many oil tankers on the seas!

Idea: Walk or take public transit instead of driving when you can!

Let's Clean the Beaches

Don't leave any trash on the beach, and try to pick up any rubbish that others may have left. Normally trashcans are provided for public use. When traveling on a boat, never throw any garbage into the water.

THE OCEANS—GIANT RUBBISH DUMPS?

If we could empty the oceans and see what's hidden there, we'd make some incredible discoveries. Doubtless we would see wrecked ships that have lain undisturbed for hundreds of years. But we would also see piles of rubbish. The Mediterranean, for instance, receives about six million items of miscellaneous garbage every day, and at any one time there are 750 million items floating on the surface. They didn't all come from ships! Three-quarters of this garbage came from the land.

Wherever there are people there is garbage. In some places, garbage isn't properly dealt with—there are no conventional dumps, no incineration, and no recycling—and everything ends up in the natural environment. The trash blows about in the wind, and much of it is washed into the rivers and ends up in the sea. If we do nothing about it, the sea is the final destination for most of our trash.

WHAT HAPPENS TO AIR POLLUTION?

As the rain comes down, it becomes contaminated with toxic elements like mercury and lead (from factory smoke and vehicle exhaust), which are suspended in the air and in turn pollute the planet's seas. All this pollution threatens marine life. Chemical substances imported by the rain affect the health of certain members of the whale family. Meanwhile the solid trash that floats on the sea surface threatens sea animals like seals, dolphins, and birds, which can swallow it and suffocate. Don't forget the planet needs your help, even during vacations!

Idea: Don't dump your trash in the ocean!

Chapter 6
Breathing Fresh Air

Mmm! The pure air of the mountains! Yes, but don't go too high. For at high altitudes there is less and less oxygen, and it becomes harder and harder to breathe. The best air for us is the air below the mountains. So long as it isn't polluted by automobiles and industry.

Safeguarding
the Ozone Layer

If you buy an aerosol (a deodorant, maybe, or hairspray), make sure it says that it is "ozone friendly." And ask your parents about the ecological rating of their refrigerator. Many refrigerators, especially older models, contain gases that are destructive for the ozone layer.

HOW DOES THE EARTH PROTECT US FROM THE SUN?

The earth is surrounded by a gas envelope called the atmosphere. It contains, among other things, a layer of ozone (a natural gas), which acts like a screen, protecting living species (humans, animals, and plants) from the sun's harmful rays. Without that shield, the earth would be exposed to the types of ultraviolet rays that cause skin cancer and eye diseases. These harmful rays also reduce photosynthesis (whereby plants absorb carbon dioxide and give out oxygen) and disrupt (or rather stop completely) the formation of plankton, the marine microorganisms that are vital to the food chain and the ecological balance of the seas.

The ozone layer is therefore a protective screen that is essential to all life on Earth. But in 1985, the world was horrified to learn from scientists that a hole had opened up in the ozone layer above Antarctica. It wasn't a "hole" as such, but rather an area where the ozone layer had become abnormally thin. The anomaly was thought to be very serious, and the culprit was quickly found: the chlorofluorocarbons (CFCs) that were used in aerosols, refrigerators, and fire extinguishers. The CFC gases were quickly replaced by equivalents that did not damage the ozone layer. This is a great example of people just like you rallying, getting involved, and making a change.

The damage was thus limited, and catastrophe was avoided. We can make a difference—we just need to not only try but also remain vigilant.

Idea: Get involved. People can actually make a difference if they rally together to change something.

Let's Get on Our Bikes

Bikes don't pollute, aren't noisy, take up little road space, and are good for your health. They're ideal for short trips. So use a bike and encourage your parents to do the same. Or, try Rollerblades!

WHAT ARE THE EFFECTS OF URBAN POLLUTION?

Respiratory illnesses (chronic bronchitis, asthma, sinusitis) are increasingly common in towns because of air pollution—especially the gases emitted by the large numbers of vehicles using the roads. The average car emits three times its weight in pollutants—several tons comprising various substances—every year. Traffic also makes a great deal of noise, which can be draining and unhealthy, even if its effects remain largely hidden. All over the world, automobiles cause major congestion, and it is estimated that the average European spends two years of his or her life in traffic jams! What a waste of time! Traffic is also a huge contributor to global warming because of the carbon dioxide it gives off: the greenhouse gas that is contained in vehicle exhaust.

WHAT CAN WE DO TO LIMIT THIS POLLUTION?

In London, Great Britain's capital city, as well as Boston, MA, the authorities are trying to discourage traffic from coming into the city center by imposing tolls and speed limits while giving priority to public transport and vehicles with more than one occupant. It is equally possible to produce vehicles that do not pollute. In Brazil, 90 percent of cars are powered by ethanol, a biofuel made from sugarcane. There are also "hybrid" cars that use gasoline outside of urban areas, but electricity within the city, and whose batteries are recharged by the car's own movement. There's no shortage of ideas and possibilities.

Idea: Think about all of the alternative methods of transportation or ways to power your car and pick the environment-friendly option that best suits your family's needs.

Every day each of us breathes about four thousand gallons of air. Since 1950, emissions of carbon dioxide have gone up four-fold, affecting the quality of the air and causing the deaths of eighty thousand Europeans each year. We ought to remember that, as we slowly alter the composition of the air, we are slowly poisoning ourselves. (source: WHO)

Chapter 7
Consuming Differently

With up-to-date farming techniques, the earth could feed twelve billion inhabitants. So why are eight hundred million people in the world still hungry? (source: FAO)

Organic farming accounts for only 2 percent of the world's surface area currently under cultivation. (source: Observatoire National de l'Agriculture Biologique, Paris)

Putting Organic Food on Our Plates

If you buy organic food, it will encourage organic agriculture, which is better for your health and for the environment. Organic milk, bread, eggs, cereals, and vegetables—there's plenty of choice!

BIRDS UNDER THREAT FROM HUMAN BEINGS

Why is it that there are fewer wild birds in our fields and gardens? The answer is: intensive agriculture. To make cultivation easier and increase crop yields, farmers have enlarged their fields and cut down the hedges and copses that the birds need for food and shelter.

How come in certain regions, like Brittany in France, there are regular warnings not to drink the domestic water supply? The reason is the same: intensive agriculture. To kill the insects that spoil their crops, farmers use pesticides, and to increase the size of their crops they use fertilizers. But the quantities of those products applied to the fields are so excessively large that the plants cannot absorb them all. When it rains, the excessive amounts of pesticides and fertilizers go directly into the groundwater and rivers from which our drinking water is taken.

IS ENVIRONMENT-FRIENDLY FARMING POSSIBLE?

Despite its bad effects on the environment (like diminishing wildlife and water pollution) and on human health—think of BSE (bovine spongiform encephalopathy, or "mad cow disease")—intensive agriculture is everywhere.

But there is a more environmentally friendly method of farming that pollutes less, uses fewer chemicals, and is more careful about animal welfare. It is what we call "organic" agriculture. Currently, "organic" produce costs more than produce grown using chemicals. But as more and more organic food is produced, prices will gradually come down.

Idea: Eat organic; it will benefit your body and the planet.

Let's Vote for an "Organic" School

In some schools, students protect the environment ... while eating! Talk to your parents—they can suggest to your school that it serve organic food, which encourages farmers who respect the environment.

DO YOU KNOW WHERE YOUR FAVORITE BURGERS COME FROM?

On the weekend, when you shop with your family, perhaps you sometimes eat in a fast-food restaurant. It's fun piling hamburgers and fries onto your plate, eating ice cream, and washing it all down with a soda, and you don't think too much about it. But unfortunately there is a dark side to this meal. The companies that sell fast foods buy their basic foodstuffs (meat, bread, cheese) in huge quantities, a practice that keeps the prices down but that is not consistent with high quality. Regular chickens, for instance, are cheaper than certified free-range chickens and are much less tasty. The food the fast-food outlets use comes from intensive agriculture, which produces large quantities at low prices but pollutes the environment and groundwater with fertilizers and chemical treatments. That's the sort of agriculture you encourage when you buy fast food.

FAST FOOD: A GIANT WASTE-MAKER

Have you ever looked at your plate at the end of a fast-food meal—the packaging, the containers, and the cups made of plastic, polystyrene, or cardboard? Just imagine the mountains of nonreclyclable garbage a fast-food outlet produces in one day, let alone a year!

Despite their faults, fast-food restaurants are as popular as ever and don't seem ready to change their ways. Unfortunately, fast food that respects the environment still seems to be a long way off.

Idea: Avoid fast-food restaurants.

Give Your Toys a New Lease on Life

Give your old toys to those who don't have any. You could donate them to organizations that will redistribute them. Or you could give them to a local playgroup or kindergarten or to a children's hospital.

HAVE YOU EVER THOUGHT ABOUT SHARING YOUR TOYS?

There must be some toys you haven't used for ages and that you don't care about anymore. Not surprising, because you're growing older. It's a shame for them to just gather dust on your bedroom shelves or sit in their boxes.

There is a child somewhere who has had fewer toys in his or her life than you and who would enjoy playing with them. Maybe he or she isn't very far away. Needy children don't just live in distant countries. In our prosperous world we tend to buy new things all the time and forget those who have nothing. Giving things away is a move in the opposite direction, toward a world of greater solidarity—a gesture that is vital if we are to save the planet! If people are not generous enough to help needy people in their own neighborhoods today, there is little chance they will be generous enough to safeguard the earth for the generations that are to come.

Of course it isn't easy to part with things, especially toys! But isn't a toy's purpose to entertain a child? Encourage yourself with that thought! You'll be pleased afterward. And you may find that you don't really miss it so very much after all.

Idea: Recycle your toys!

Let's Borrow Instead of Buy

Every week choose new toys by borrowing them from your local toy library, just as you would a book. Make some inquiries. If there isn't a toy library in your district, maybe you could request that your community set one up!

WHY BUY WHEN YOU CAN BORROW?

You don't always have to buy what you want. The custom of buying—always buying—great quantities of things (that sometimes end up being little used) is part of what is called "the consumer society." Over the last thirty years, people in the wealthy nations have been encouraged to buy more and more things. Our houses are increasingly filled with all kinds of equipment, our closets and wardrobes are overflowing, and our cars are ever newer and more powerful. And to keep pace with the explosion in consumption, the factories that turn out these goods are running at full tilt! But making all these products uses huge amounts of raw materials taken from nature, as well as water and energy, and it uses harmful substances that pollute the air and water. It's another reason why our planet isn't doing too well.

Just as public libraries ensure that books are read and reread by lots of people, a toy library ensures that toys are enjoyed by a maximum number of children, and that full use is made of the valuable resources that have gone into making them. With toy libraries you don't need to manufacture ten toys for ten children. One is enough!

Idea: Borrow something, whether it's a toy or a book. You'll save your family the cost of buying something new, and you'll help the environment at the same time.

More than 30 percent of children in developing countries—about six hundred million—live on less than one U.S. dollar a day. A third of the world's population has no electricity. More than one hundred million children get no schooling. (source: UNICEF)

Buy Fair Trade

At the supermarket, opt for products labeled "fair trade." It's a guarantee that they have been produced in good working conditions.

EQUAL RIGHTS FOR ALL?

Elsewhere in the world, there are children your age who do not go to school. Instead of sitting in a classroom, they spend their days working on plantations, picking fruit, sewing, or plying small trades in the street. Many live in poverty and do not have proper clothing or toys. Some are even made to fight in wars. That's their life. It isn't an easy one.

HOW DO WE HELP THESE DEPRIVED CHILDREN?

Maybe you can't do this directly. But you can do small things to help the world change and become a more just place. Certain foodstuffs, including coffee, tea, bananas, and cocoa, come from abroad where peasant farmers don't earn enough to

house, clothe, and feed themselves properly, let alone go to the doctor and send their children to school. If you buy imported goods—chocolate, bananas, orange juice, pineapples, honey, sugar, tea, clothes, toys—bearing a "fair trade" label, you'll be making sure they've been fairly produced, with adequate pay for labor, reasonable working conditions, and without child labor. The more people buy "fair trade" products, the fairer international trade will become. It's just a few cents and dollars extra for us at the cash register. But for the producer at the other end it's life-changing.

Idea: Pay attention to labels—buy things marked "fair trade."

Look for the Ecolabel

Do you know the Energy Star label? You can find it on electrical items for sale in America, Europe, and elsewhere in the world. It means that the product, be it a dishwasher, hot water heater, or even a new house, meets strict energy efficiency guidelines laid down by the U.S. Environmental Protection Agency and the U.S. Department of Energy. European Union products increasingly bear a blue flower symbol, indicating to the consumer that their manufacturer used a minimum of virgin natural resources and that the products are mainly recyclable.

WHERE DO THE PRODUCTS WE BUY COME FROM?

When people buy clothing, what they look for most is the label and how fashionable it is. They rarely wonder about the social and environmental aspects of its manufacture.

Who made it? In what country? How much were they paid? What material is it made of? Did its manufacture cause pollution? Did its production use a lot of energy? Is the packaging recyclable? In order to make it available here, did its production encourage excessive exploitation of natural resources in a poor country? If you knew the answers to questions like these, you'd be able to judge whether the product you're interested in was friendly to the environment and the human beings who made it. But such answers are not easy to find.

THAT'S WHY ECOLABELS ARE SO USEFUL.

Ecolabels can tell you whether the production of an item has respected the environment and the people who produced it. Different countries have different labels, and some labels, like the FSC (Forest Stewardship Council) tree logo, are international. The FSC logo certifies that the wood used in a product has come from a sustainably managed forest. Up-to-date details of this and other logos used in the United States and elsewhere can be found at www.greenerchoices.org. Ecolabeled goods are not necessarily more expensive than their nonecological equivalents.

Idea: The types of products you buy make all the difference, so why not buy ones that are environmentally responsible? Look for the Ecolabel!

Join in Buy Nothing Day

Every year, at the end of November—the last Friday (United States) or Saturday (Europe)—Buy Nothing Day is a good opportunity to think about excessive consumption and the difference between "needing" things and "wanting" them. Why not join in and encourage your family to do the same?

THE DIFFERENCE BETWEEN NEEDING AND WANTING

We're so easily tempted by goods we "want." If we have enough money, we buy them, without ever wondering whether we really "need" them. We buy huge amounts of things like clothes and shoes that we never wear, sporting goods and tools that we almost never use, toys that sit in closets, and poor-quality, cheap goods that break as soon as we use them.

Purchases of this sort all contribute to the general squandering of the world's natural resources, to needless pollution, and to the world's ever-growing mountains of garbage. It is a pattern of consumption found mainly in the world's richest countries, where on average one child consumes as much of the world's resources and creates as much pollution as forty children born in a poor country. If everyone in the world consumed as we do, we would need two extra planets!

What we seem to be saying to the inhabitants of the world's poorest countries is this: It's better for you to stay poor, because the earth can't supply everyone or absorb all the pollution that would be created. That's the reality. But is it right? Doesn't it make more sense for us in the wealthier countries to make changes in the way we live?

Idea: Cut down on consumerism! Have a Buy Nothing Day once a month.

Jules Renard: "On earth there is no heaven, but there are pieces of it."
(Journal, December 28, 1896)

Vincent van Gogh to his brother Theo: "*Admire* as much as you can; most people *don't admire enough.*"

(London, January 1874, tr. Johanna van Gogh-Bonger)

Sort Through Your Wardrobe

Is your wardrobe overflowing with clothes? Give what you never wear to organizations that collect clothes for redistribution to needy people here and abroad. Some local authorities have special containers in which you can place used clothes. You could also organize a roundup of old clothes in your class or school.

CLOTHES MANUFACTURING USES NATURAL RESOURCES...
... and sometimes it causes serious damage. For example, in Kazakhstan, the Aral Sea has shrunk to half its size, marooning on the desert sand the boats that used to fish in its waters. It is cotton-growing that has caused the disaster. To irrigate that thirsty crop, the authorities diverted two large rivers that used to run into the sea, and they have also used large quantities of pesticides. The result? The sea's coastline has retreated some fifty miles, and the environment has been polluted with chemicals, emptying it of the animal species that once lived there.

These days it is possible to find clothes made from organic cotton. This is cotton grown in an environmentally friendly way and processed in textile factories where less polluting dyes are used.

So that's why it's important to give your clothes as long a life as possible by passing them on to others when you've finished wearing them. Especially if they could really use them. Do you know that about 85 percent of textiles (clothes, bed linens, and other items) are simply thrown away and destroyed with the household garbage?

Idea: Share your old clothing; give it another life and home (not the trashcan!).

Let's Go Green at Our Schools!

If you'd like your school to be at the forefront of environmental protection, you could suggest that it join the international network of Eco-Schools. There are already twenty thousand of them across forty countries. It's a way of making lots of friends!

IS IT POSSIBLE FOR A SCHOOL TO BE GREEN?

Can you imagine a school where old batteries are collected so that they don't pollute the environment? where garbage is sorted for recycling? where litter is cleared up? where drinking water is economized by recycling rainwater? where the buildings have solar panels to limit global warming? where travel is only by bike to avoid air pollution? where leftovers are composted to make fertilizer? where energy is saved by heating the rooms conservatively and fitting the corridor lights with timed switches? In short, a school that applies the sort of day-to-day concrete solutions that will really make a difference for the planet?

Well, school isn't like home. There are a lot more people to convince. It isn't easy to get things to change. You don't know where to begin? OK, there's little anyone can do on their own. But there is a way of mobilizing the whole school—staff, management, and students. It's the international Eco-School program. Mention it to your teacher and help to make yours a green school!

Idea: Apply some or all of these ideas to your daily life, and get involved in any and every way you can. YOU can make the difference!

Rio Earth Summit,
© Ribeiro Antonio/Gamma

Sossusvlei Sand Dunes,
Namibia

Cranberry factory, USA

White Desert, Egypt

Bristlecone pines, USA

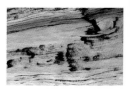
Bristlecone pine (detail),
USA

Fjorland National Park,
New Zealand

Blue Lagoon, Iceland

Geyser, Yellowstone
National Park, USA

Green tortoise, Australia

Giant cuttlefish, Great
Barrier Reef, Australia

Humpback whales,
Polynesia

Gorgonian coral,
Great Barrier Reef, Australia

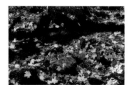
Maple leaves, Acadia
National Park, USA

Vaccination campaign,
Colombia

Boreal forest, Finland

Frost, Sweden

Olympic National Park, USA

Amazon Rain Forest,
French Guiana

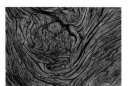
Tree trunk (detail), USA

Namib Desert, Namibia

Sequoia National Park, USA

Clownfish, Great Barrier
Reef, Australia

Marine iguana, Galapagos
Islands

Elephant, Amboseli
National Park, Kenya

Niger River, Mali

Water lily, Mali

Red ibis, Venezuela

Bacteria, Kamchatka, Russia

Elk, Rocky Mountain
National Park, USA

Sequoias in the mist,
Redwood National Park,
USA

Japanese cranes

Amazon Rain Forest,
French Guiana

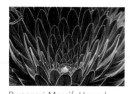
Rwenzori Massif, Uganda

Pine bark, USA

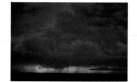
Storm on the Great Plains,
USA

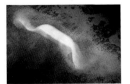
Nautilus, Great Barrier Reef, Australia

Coral island, Australia

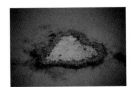
Great Barrier Reef, Australia

Osprey Reef, Australia

Glacial melt channel, Greenland

Beached ice, Iceland

Sastrugi, Antarctica

Emperor penguin, Antarctica

Steelworks at dusk, © Luis Veiga/Getty Images

Caymans, Venezuela

Birth of a tornado, Great Plains, USA

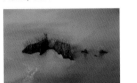
Hawaii, USA

Coral reefs at low tide, Australia

Frog on cranberries, USA

Flamingo, Lake Nakuru, Kenya

Sandbanks, Bahamas

Acid Lake, Vanuatu

River, Iceland

Torrent, Greenland

Hot springs, Yellowstone National Park, USA

Well, Mauritania

Humpback whale, Polynesia

Atlantic puffin, Iceland

Shoal of barracuda, Australia

Cape Farewell, Southern Greenland

Clouds, Hawaii, USA

Iceberg, Antarctica

Cranberries, USA

Wild grasses in a field, USA

Child playing, South Africa, © David Turnley/Corbis

Kilauea volcano, Hawaii, USA

Sunrise, Mali

Herd, Sahara Desert, Niger

Fula nomads' household effects, Niger

Weddell seal, Antarctica

Gray whale, Mexico

Library of Congress Cataloging-in-Publication Data

Jankeliowitch, Anne.
50 ways to save the earth / by Anne Jankéliowitch ; photographs by Philippe Bourseiller.
p. cm.
Includes bibliographical references and index.
ISBN 978-0-8109-7239-1
(Harry N. Abrams : alk. paper)
1. Environmental protection—Citizen participation.
2. Conservation of natural resources—Citizen participation.
I. Bourseiller, Philippe. II.
Title. III. Title: Fifty ways to save the earth.

TD171.7.J36 2008
333.72—dc22
2007044459

Book design by Elisabeth Ferté
Translated by Graham Robert Edwards

Copyright © 2007 Éditions de la Martinière
English translation copyright © 2008 Abrams Books for Young Readers

Abrams Books for Young Readers are available at special discounts when purchased in quantity for premiums and promotions as well as fundraising or educational use. Special editions can also be created to specification. For details, contact specialmarkets@hnabooks.com or the address below.

Printed and bound in China
10 9 8 7 6 5 4 3 2

ABRAMS
THE ART OF BOOKS SINCE 1949

115 West 18th Street
New York, NY 10011
www.abramsbooks.com